THE
Archive Photographs
SERIES

THE
POTTERIES

A group of saggar maker's bottom knockers, photographed in 1921. They used a large wooden tool known as a "maul" to compress clay within a metal ring to make the saggar base.

THE
Archive Photographs
SERIES
THE
POTTERIES

Compiled by
Ian Lawley

THE
CHALFORD
PRESS
BATH • AUGUSTA • RENNES

First published 1994
Copyright © Ian Lawley, 1994

The Chalford Press
12 Riverside Court
Bath BA2 3DZ

ISBN 0 7524 0046 0

Typesetting and origination by
The Chalford Press
Printed in Great Britain by
Redwood Books, Trowbridge

Stephen Liversage's pawnbroker's shop, Furlong Parade, Burslem, c.1900. Many working class families only managed to balance their household budgets with the aid of the pawnbroker. There were at least forty pawnbrokers in the Potteries at this time.

Contents

Acknowledgements

The majority of photographs in this book are taken from the photographic archives of the City Museum and Art Gallery, Stoke-on-Trent, and the Gladstone Working Pottery Museum. A number are taken from the Hartshill Photograph Collection, which was put together by the Hartshill Festival Committee during the 1970s. I would like to thank all the many individuals who have given photographs to these collections.

Special thanks for permission to reproduce photographs go to Ray Johnson, who provided still images from a number of early films, Helen Trelfa, Christine Wood, Miss Gladys Moss, Mr. S. Kirkham and Mr. R. Morrey.

I would also like to thank Andrew Dobraszczyc, Angela Lee, Ray Johnson, Liz Salmon, Pat Halfpenny, Jenine Evans, Kathy Niblett, Deb Skinner, Alan Taylor and Allan Townsend for information; Richard Weston and David Simcock for photographic work; Sharon Cooper and Judith Billing, for their word processing skills; Kate Lawley, for her patience; and all my colleagues at the City Museum and Art Gallery. Any errors are my own.

In memory of Stan Moody (1924-1994), a regular visitor to the Potteries.

Introduction

The North Staffordshire Potteries are the only area in Britain to be so completely identified with one industry. The presence of the ceramics industry has played a dominant role in shaping both the economic life and the landscape of the area. The lives of local people have been played out against what Arnold Bennett described as "a singular scenery of coal dust, potshards, flame and steam".

This collection of photographs attempts to illuminate the everyday life of this remarkable area during the past one hundred years. As well as illustrating people at work and on the move within the distinctive urban environment of Stoke-on-Trent, these images have been selected to give some impression of the sense of community felt by Potteries people. One sequence of photographs illustrates the important social role played by the churches and chapels of the area. Although their attendances may have been declining, they continued to organise a wide range of community activities, including clubs and societies, football matches, concert parties, sewing circles and carnivals, as well as providing a focus for charitable work. Sport provided another important social bond. Sporting photographs included here depict everything from school p.e. drill to cycle clubs, as well as football, "the people's game". It is interesting to note that Stoke-on-Trent produced a highly effective ladies team at the beginning of the 1920s. Sadly, the strong opposition to the notion of girls playing football which existed then still persists today.

In an area where family incomes were often low, much of the entertainment on offer was home-grown. Amateur drama, choral societies, bands, pageants and carnivals flourished in the Potteries. The City's parks, "the lungs of the people" as they were known, provided pleasure for thousands of local families. Although there were attempts to promote "worthy" recreational pursuits, such as horticulture, many working people preferred to look forward to events such as the traditional annual wakes. Together with other calendar festivals, holiday excursions, royal visits and other popular celebrations, these occasions brought a dash of welcome colour to the Potteries Landscape.

The photographs in this book came from two main sources, the photographic archive of the City Museum and Art Gallery, and the collections of the Gladstone Pottery Museum. Most of the photographs have been given to the two museums by local people, or loaned for copying. As far as possible, I have tried to avoid photographs which are already in wide circulation. Most of these images are published here for the first time, with the aim of making them accessible to a wider audience. Together, they reflect the interest that the museums have in recording the lives and experience of Potteries People.

Ian Lawley
November 1994

One
Potteries People

A pottery family in their back yard, Burslem, c.1900. This is one of a series of photographs taken by the Reverend M.A. Graham, Archdeacon of Stoke-on-Trent, and his curate, the Reverend A.E.M. Stanham, at the close of the nineteenth century.

Boys and girls in the grounds of the Mount School for the Blind and Deaf, Penkhull, c.1900.

Left: Two brothers, c.1905. The boy on the left became a miner and died of pneumoconiosis. He was buried on Armistice Day, 1918. His brother ran away to sea. Both boys were brought up at the Penkhull Children's Homes, which opened in around 1900.

Right: "A father to many, but none his own". This former soldier, photographed at Shelton in 1946, was already stepfather to six daughters when he adopted a three week old abandoned baby.

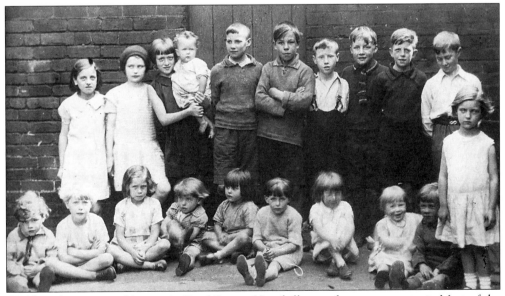

Children from terraced houses in Steel Street, Hartshill, pose for a street portrait. Most of the houses in the street, which was built during the 1830s, were demolished in 1958.

The staff of Hartshill School, probably including the headmaster, Thomas Beswick, c.1910. The school, which stands behind Hartshill Church, was opened in 1852 and was extended in the 1890s to cater for the needs of an expanding population. It eventually closed in 1964.

Working with clay, c.1950. Pupils at Broom Street School, Hanley, take part in a craft class.

Girls at Moorland Road Domestic Centre, Burslem, 1926. Training in cookery, laundry-work and "home-craft" was provided for girls of twelve and over at a number of domestic centres throughout the city.

Boys gardening, c.1922. Many local schools began to run their own gardens during the 1914–1918 war. As many families had neither a garden nor an allotment, this provided some children with their first and only experience of horticulture. By the early 1920s more than half the City's schools had their own gardens.

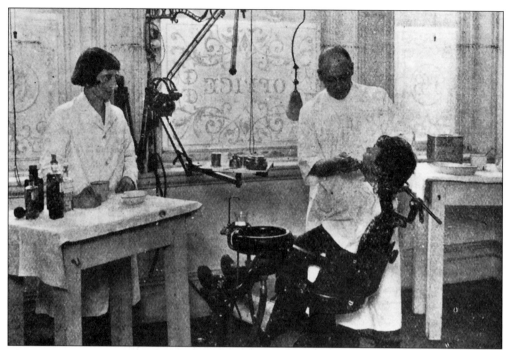

The School Dentist, c.1923. The School Medical Service provided routine dental inspection for all children in the City aged between six and eight. In 1923 the school Dentist examined the teeth of 6,505 local children and treated nearly 3,000 for "dental defects".

Children in the Open Air Ward at the Orthopaedic Hospital, Hartshill. The Orthopaedic Hospital was established at Longfield Cottage by the Cripples Aid Society in 1919, but soon became overcrowded. Temporary buildings were erected in the grounds in the early 1920s and a new Orthopaedic Hospital eventually opened in 1931.

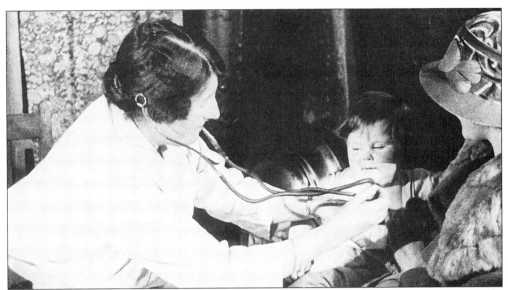

Medical examination, 1926. A doctor listens to a child's chest at the Burslem Medical Centre. At this time, nearly a quarter of all deaths in the Potteries were caused by respiratory disease.

Life study, Burslem School of Art, c.1950. A student mixes colour on her palette. Burslem was a centre of art for the City, providing full and part-time training for ceramic designers and modellers as well as classes in fine art, graphic design and dress-making.

Sea Cadets, 1950. The cadets spent a week on board the training ship H.M.S. Modeste. One of these boys, Cadet Leading Seaman L. Cotterill (second row, second on the left) was chosen from hundreds of Cadets to take part in the Empire Sea Cadet Camp in Montreal. The Cadets met each week in Victoria Square, Shelton.

Left: Gunner William Thomas Beeston on horseback, Shelton, c.1914.
Right: Amos Burton (seated) and two unidentified officers, 1914–1918 War. Burton left his post as Stoke-on-Trent's Borough Engineer and Surveyor to enlist, returning at the end of the war.

Outcropping at Meir Hay. This is one of a number of photographs taken during the coal dispute of 1912 showing striking miners and their families picking coal.

Back alley way, 1920s. An arched passage leads into the alley, which is lined with outside toilets.

Left: Oliver Lodge (1851–1940), the first man to transmit a message by radio telegraphy. This photograph was taken in 1889 when the Penkull-born Scientist was professor of physics and mathematics at University College, Liverpool.

Right: William Woodall, M.P. (1832–1901). Formerly a Burslem councillor, Woodall was Liberal M.P. for Stoke-on-Trent from 1880 to 1885, after which he represented Hanley.

Isaac Cook, caretaker at the Wedgwood Museum, Burslem. The museum opened to the public in May 1906 under the watchful eye of Cook, who had been with the firm for fifty-one years.

Left: Arnold Bennett (1867–1931) in 1907. Although Bennett left Staffordshire to work in London when he was twenty-one, the Potteries remained his principal source of inspiration.
Right: James Maddock, pottery manufacturer and philanthropist, 1890. In 1887 Maddock contributed £1,000 to build an extension to the Wedgwood Institute, Burslem. As mayor he presented the drinking fountain in St. John's Square.

Ramsay MacDonald visits the Potteries, 1924. Samuel Clowes (seated, far left), who began his working life as a mouldrunner at Cauldon Pottery, became the first pottery worker to enter Parliament when he was elected M.P. for Hanley in 1924. Arthur Hollins (standing, third from left) was General Secretary of the National Society of Pottery Workers. Andrew MacLaren (seated, far right) also became a Labour M.P.

Members of the Longton Fire Brigade pose with their horse-drawn engine, in front of Louis Taylor's showroom, Commerce Street, Longton.

Cobridge Fire Brigade, c.1890. Burslem was served by three fire engines, at Longport, Burslem, and Cobridge.

Group portrait showing members of Hanley's police force in 1895. The borough force was set up in 1870 and from 1884 was based in the Town Hall in Albion Street.

Workmen at the Atlas Foundry in Hanley pose for a group photograph, 1904. The owners were Gosling and Gatensbury.

W.J. Shenton's Cratemaker's Yard, Lower Spring Street, Longton, 1926. A group of Cratemakers pose in their aprons.

Bob Nixon, fireman, photographed at work at one of the calcining kilns, Mintons, c.1930.

Flint grinders at J. Aynsley and Sons Portland Mill, c.1900. This photograph was taken by George Pickin, whose father managed the works.

A group of workmen in the the yard of Joseph Emery's Grange Street Works, Cobridge, c.1900. This colour manufacturing business was founded in 1845.

The chemical laboratory at Wenger's Colour Works, c.1900. The firm manufactured colours and chemicals for the ceramics industry. In 1900, Wengers opened a new factory at Etruria, equipped with state of the art laboratories.

The General Office, Furnival's Works, Cobridge, 1913.

The North Staffordshire Steam Laundry, Basford, c.1915. Established in 1875, this was one of several laundries serving the needs of the area's relatively small middle class. Boasting that 'high class work is our watchword', the firm offered special facilities for "brushing and pressing gentlemen's suits and overcoats and ladies' woollen costumes".

P. White, Dairyman, and assistant, with his hand cart, c.1914. They delivered milk to families in the Penkhull and Newcastle area. His young companion is holding a metal pail, which would be filled from the large churn fixed to the centre of the cart.

Counting banknotes, Trentham Gardens, c.1940. During the Second World War the Assembly Rooms were used as a central clearing bank.

Two

The Pottery Towns

Tunstall Town Hall, c.1910. To the left of the main entrance is the Criterion Restaurant, to the right W.H. Bailey and Sons and Naylor's Bon Marché, a clothing store. The Town Hall was completed in 1885 on the High Street, facing the Market Square.

Market Square, Tunstall, with single deck buses, c.1928. Two rival firms, the Potteries Electric Traction Company and the Associated North Staffs Bus Proprietors, operated services at this time.

Porthill in the snow, c.1900. This photograph was taken on a glass negative with a field camera set on a tripod.

Newcastle Street, Middleport, looking towards Burslem, 1918. This image is taken from a feature-length film, "A Pottery Girl's Romance", which was made for William Rhodes, manager of Burslem Picture Palace. It was a common sight to see lads walking barefoot. Harry Hood stands in the foreground, wearing a large cap.

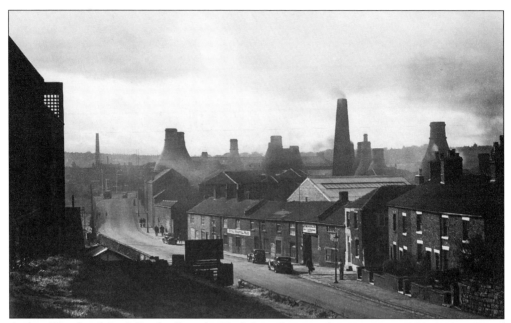

Arthur Wood and Son's Bradwell works, Trubshaw Cross, early morning, c.1950. Arthur Wood and Son used the trade name "Royal Bradwell" from around 1945.

Newcastle Street, Burslem, looking towards the Town Hall, 1920s. A well-dressed man is pushing a pram along the street.

Alcock, Lindley and Bloore's Ascot Pottery, c.1950. Established in 1919, this works mainly produced teapots. It was acquired by the Allied English Pottery Group in 1959.

J. Todd's chemist shop, Newcastle Street, Burslem, c.1900. This photograph is taken from a collection of glass negatives which were found at the shop.

The Wedgwood Institute, Burslem, c.1900. The foundation stone was laid by the Chancellor of the Exchequer, William Gladstone, in 1863 and the building opened in 1869. Built as a memorial to Josiah Wedgwood, the institute housed a school of art, lecture theatre, museum, reading room and library. The front of the institute is decorated with terra cotta and mosaic panels depicting the months of the year and the signs of the Zodiac.

Burslem Town Hall and Meat Market, c.1955. The Meat Market, which was built in 1836, was demolished in 1958.

Berryhill Brick-works and colliery. By 1930 this had become one of the largest suppliers of brick in the Midlands, quarrying 2,000 tons of clay each week. The works also supplied clay for local pottery manufacturers.

Shelton colliery pit head, c.1960. Once the deepest pit in North Staffordshire, its underground galleries extended to Stoke. In 1957, by which time it was the only working pit in Hanley, the colliery employed 750 men underground and 290 men above ground.

Hanley roof tops. This photograph, from the Gladstone Pottery Museum's archives is believed to have been taken in the 1930s. It is one of many smoky views of the Potteries taken in the days before the Clean Air Act of 1950.

The north side of the Market Square, Hanley, c.1890. Robinson's shop, on the corner of Swan Passage, was demolished in 1891.

Theo Hughes, Signwriter's Shop and Plumber's Yard, Hanley, 1914. The *Sentinel* Offices are on the left. A bill poster reads, "Austrians Advancing on Germany".

Looking up Picadilly from Broad Street, Hanley, 1912.

Stafford Street, Hanley, c.1910. The posters above Teeton's Shop front advertise ladies' corsets. This drapers and haberdasher's shop, which was established during the 1860s, stocked a wide range of clothing, footwear, and dress material.

Charles Ede and Co., Wholesale Ironmongers, 73 Stafford Street, Hanley, c.1895. This long-established business held extensive stocks of cutlery, stoves, furnishings, gas fittings, tools and builders' materials.

Left: Stewarts Warehouses, New Street, Hanley, 1890s. This wholesale ironmongers boasted the largest collections of ranges, grates and builders' ironmongery in the Midlands.
Right: William Rowlands and his son George at their shop on the corner of Town Road and Lower Mayer Street, Hanley.

Twyfords Cliffe Vale Potteries. Praised by the factory inspectors as a Model Factory, the sanitary ware works were built alongside the canal and had their own railway sidings.

The Chemical Works, Etruria Gas Works, 1926. In 1924 a scheme was agreed with the Unemployment Grants Committee to engage unemployed local people to construct a Chemical Works at Etruria. The works, which opened at the end of 1926, included tar distillation and sulphate of ammonia plants.

Gas Works, Wharf Street, Stoke. These works were established in 1843. By 1920, much of the plant was outdated and production costs were high. It was decided to centralise gas production at Etruria on the site of the British Gas Light Company's works.

Stoke Station, c.1925. Stoke had been the headquarters of the North Staffordshire Railway, whose operations had been taken over by the L.M.S. In 1930, a first class single fare from Stoke to London (Euston) was 30s 6d.

Hartshill Road, c.1912. Richard Heath acquired the franchise to run a post office in his grocer's shop on the corner of Cumming Street in about 1910. This shop formed part of a group of buildings known as "The Prince of Wales Place".

Stoke Old Road, 1960s. A group of children walk past the terraced houses on their way to school.

High Street, Stoke, 1908. Alfred Birks draper's shop is on the right. This business was established in the mid-1880s and by 1898 Alfred Birks was able to afford a large house in Queens Road, Penkhull.

Molloys Fishmongers, Fruiterers and Poulterers, High Street, Stoke, c.1890. The Shop was taken over by Frank Toft in 1889. During the next few years he installed refrigerators "with a consuming capacity of ten tons of ice weekly". Fresh fish was supplied daily from Grimsby.

Fire damage to Alfred Birks drapers shop, High Street, Stoke. A crowd has gathered to view the gutted shop premises, which were later rebuilt.

Left: Johnson's shop, Hartshill Road, late 1920s. Herbert Johnson and his son, Walter, are standing in the doorway.
Right: Baskets on the pavement outside Johnson's shop, Hartshill Road.

Footbridge over the Newcastle Canal, Stoke. The Villas, a group of Italianate houses built for local pottery manufacturers in the 1850s, can be seen across the canal to the left.

The Central Commercial Hotel, Church Street, Stoke, c.1890. Run by Mr James Hobbs, this hotel specialised in the commercial travel trade, offering its guests billiards as well as "well aired beds".

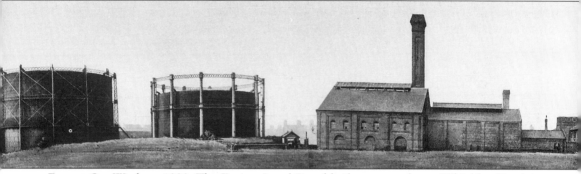

Fenton Gas Works, c.1920. The Fenton Local Board built a gas works on Whieldon Road, in 1883. The works passed into the ownership of the County Borough of Stoke-on-Trent after Federation and was eventually closed in 1924, when it was decided to centralise gas production at Etruria.

Edensor Marl Pit, c.1920. The pit has been excavated on the very edge of the town. Clay was lifted up on the rail track which can be seen in the centre of the photograph.

Station Bridge, Longton, c.1890. St. John's Church (now demolished) and the Crown Hotel are visible behind the bridge. The bridge, which carries the Stoke to Derby line, was completed in 1889.

Market Street, Longton, looking down towards the railway bridge. A horse drawn cart passes Boot's Chemist Shop.

Trade Union March, Normacot Road, Longton, *c.* 1908. A small group of people has gathered outside J.T. Kinsey's general store.

Henry Yates' Ironmongers Shop, Market Street, Longton, 1890s. This long established business specialised in agricultural implements, mechanical appliances and domestic machinery.

Horse-drawn wagon in Furnace Road, Normacot. These substantially built terraces were put up towards the end of the 19th century.

Meir Water Works, 1882. The Potteries Water Works Company took on the lease of the Duke of Sutherland's works at Meir in 1849. Further wells were sunk at Meir in the 1860s and a new pumping house installed in 1882.

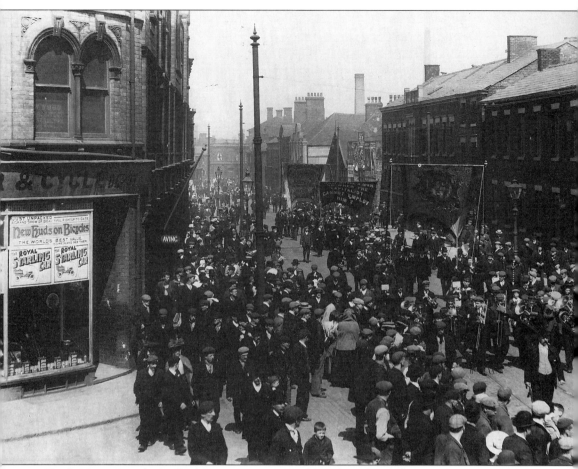

Trade Union March, Stafford Street, Longton. Led by a brass band, the marchers are carrying a series of banners. The central banner poses the question, "What shall a man do when the capitalist cannot employ him?".

Three

Working in the Potbanks

Inside the pan room, Minton's, late 1920s. Jack Adams and workmates clear out one of the grinding pans in Minton's flint mill. Calcined and crushed flint was ground to a fine powder in the pans before being used to whiten and strengthen the clay used in the pottery works.

Inside the slip house, Minton's, c.1930. Bill Adams mixes slip with a wooden plank. The clay was combined with other body ingredients in water.

Wooden filter presses, Winton Pottery. Water was forced out of the clay under pressure between filters. These were then emptied and the clay was carried to the making shop.

Mouldmaking at the Sutherland China Works, Longton. This is one of a series of glass slides that were produced by the company to illustrate china making processes. Moulds were used extensively throughout the pottery industry.

Dick Stephenson and his mould runner. A mould runner was a young person who would bring moulds to the maker and then carry the moulded items to the drying room. It might be that person's first job in the factory and would also involve many other menial but necessary tasks.

George Ratcliffe (standing on the far left) and his
mould making team. This photograph was
probably taken at Johnson Brothers' Works,
Joiner's Square, Hanley. George Ratcliffe had five
sons, who followed him into the works.

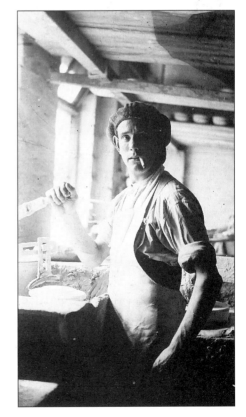

Plate-maker in an unidentified potbank. This
photograph was taken in the early part of the
century by F.W. Birks of Fenton.

Making cups at the Spode Works, Stoke. Lucretia Brookes is working a jolley, late 1920s. Clay was placed in a mould, a profile inserted to shape the interior, and the surplus clay was scraped away as the wheel turned.

Cupmaking at Mayer and Sherratts factory, Stafford Street, Longton, 1920.

9. FETTLING
SAUCERS AND PLATES

Fettling saucers and plates at the Sutherland China Works, Longton. It was the fettler's job to smooth away the seam marks left by the mould, and any other irregularities.

Lucretia Brookes, Sponger/Fettler, at Weatherby's China Works, Hanley, c.1950.

A turner at work in an unidentified pottery factory. Turning on a lathe removed the surplus clay, producing the final shape of the ware.

Teapot making team, Parrots earthenware works, Albert Street, Burslem.

Basketmaking, c.1945. A group of women workers make china baskets, probably for the export trade.

Dipping cups at the Aynsley Works, Commerce Street, Longton, c.1920. Pots were dipped by hand into a tank of liquid containing glaze ingredients. The ware was then fired to fix the glaze on the body. Dippers often became ill because the glaze mix included lead which was absorbed through the skin.

Printing onto tissue, Shelley's Foley Pottery, Longton, c.1930.

A woman applies a transfer onto a commemorative teapot, c.1900. There was a large market for cheap commemorative ware.

Saggar makers at work, John Lockett and Co., Longton, 1932. Saggars were made from a rough clay known as saggar marl. A wooden tool know as a "maul" was used to beat the clay into an iron ring until it was filled evenly, to make the saggar bottom.

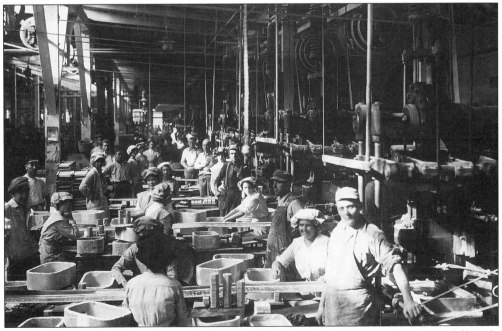

Mechanised Saggar making. In this large workshop saggar making has become a full scale industrial operation.

Placing Saggars inside the Kiln for firing, probably at the Elgin Pottery.

Operating a continuous kiln, Winton Pottery. Ware was loaded into iron crates and cranked round in a circle to the firing zone. This coke-fired enamel kiln achieved a firing temperature of 800°C.

Sorting finished goods at Gibson's Albany Pottery, Burslem. Mr Sam Gibson and Mr Lindop are standing in the centre of the warehouse, on the right. This firm was established in 1865 and moved production to Shelton in 1965.

Row of Glost ovens, Twyford's Works. Thomas Twyford opened his model factory in Cliffe Vale in 1887. It was the largest sanitary pottery works in Staffordshire, employing more than 400 people.

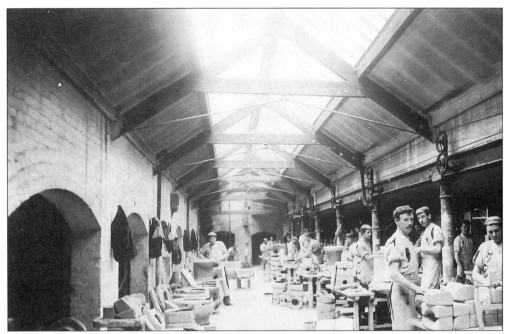

Fireclay Workshop, Cliffe Vale Pottery, c.1910. Moulds for Water Closets are stacked on the left. White enameled fireclay sanitary ware was one of the factory's principal lines of production.

Lavatory bowls stacked in the glost warehouse, Cliffe Vale Pottery. Twyford's sanitary ware gained an international reputation for quality. The Company's products were described as "absolutely the best appliances of the sort ever introduced to the market".

Saggar making by machine at Richards Tiles Pinnox Works, Woodland Street, Tunstall. This image is taken from a photograph album made by the firm in 1927 to record its work. In 1934 the company opened a new factory on the main road at Brownhills.

Women workers assembling art mosaics at the Pinnox Works, 1927. This was a time-consuming and labour intensive task.

A clay drying room at the Pinnox Works. The women are stacking tiles on shelves to dry.

A tilemaker poses alongside a tile press at an unidentified works, c.1910.

An insulator shop, c.1920. A group of women are making electrical insulators. The young woman in the foreground is checking the insulators.

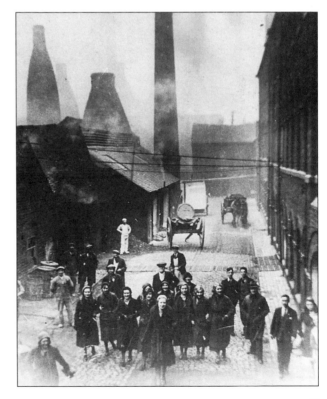

A group of pottery workers smile for the camera as they make their way out of the works. A slip wagon stands in the yard behind them.

Four pottery workers pose for the camera alongside packing crates in the yard of an unidentified potbank, c.1890. The photograph was taken by the Reverend A.E.H. Stanham.

Four

On the Move

J. Bateman's stables, Tunstall, c.1900. These working horses were hired out with their carts and drivers as carriers. In 1911, the Potteries Master Carters Association agreed to pay drivers twenty-five shillings for a sixty-hour working week.

Carriage and horse at Tunstall, c.1900. W. Moore is listed as an "omnibus proprietor" in the 1880s and 1890s. Later he is listed as a cab proprietor and supplier of horse-drawn hearses.

Horse-drawn slip cart at the Soho Mills, Station Road, Tunstall, c.1900. This sturdy working horse is decorated with brasses and a rosette.

"Our Rolling Stock", 1902. That was how the Burslem Industrial Co-operative Society described this horse and cart in a promotional booklet issued in the early years of this century.

Horse-drawn wagon belonging to J. Cliffe of Burslem leaving the Sanitary Pottery works, Longport. This photograph was taken by Mr. W. T. Vickers, who worked at the factory in the 1940s. An enthusiastic photographer, he recorded many scenes of local life.

H. Farrall, poultry dealer, pictured riding on his two wheeled horse-drawn cart. For many years the Farrall family ran a market stall in Hanley.

Horses bring crates of finished sanitary ware, packed in straw, to the railway sidings at Twyford's Cliffe Vale Works.

Old Lockett's Lane, Longton. A horse drawn cart passes by a towering kiln.

Horse-drawn carrier, Lamb Street, Hanley, c.1890. The carrier operated from the Cleveland House Stables in Shelton. The photograph was taken outside W. Jackson's Blacking Shop, a supplier of black lead.

Horse-drawn wagon belonging to M. Huntbach and Co. of Hanley, Hope Street, c.1900. The horse has been dressed for the May Festival Parade, for which it was awarded second prize.

W.J. Shenton's yard, Lower Spring Street, Longton, 1926. W.J. Shenton is holding the horse. The other man is probably his brother. Crates were made at the yard until the 1950s.

BYATT'S Motor Garage,

RING UP 178, LONGTON, For Well-Equipped TAXI CABS. Experienced Careful Drivers. Popular Charges. Estimates for Long and Short Distances.

Advertisement for Byatt's Garage, Longton. This was one of the area's earliest taxi firms.

"Three miles a penny", Kerr Stuart diesel lorry. Kerr Stuart boasted that their seven-ton diesel lorry operated at less than a tenth of the fuel cost of a similar petrol vehicle. The lorries were made at the California works, Mount Pleasant. The works had previously been occupied by a railway engineering company.

The Hanley Garage, Cheapside, c.1930. This was the main outlet for Austin and Armstrong Siddeley cars in the area.

George Pickin poses with his Penny Farthing bicycle, c.1904. George Pickin, an "engine driver" at Aynsley's Portland Mill, was a member of the St. Barnabas Cycling Club.

Mr and Mrs Welch on their tandem cycle, c.1900. This photograph was taken in the yard of 442 Waterloo Road, Cobridge.

"Mrs Hickman's grandparents riding a Centaur Convertible", 1887. The Hickmans were friends of the Welch family (pictured above).

Albert Tonkinson with his motor cycle, Wetley Rocks, 1907. Albert Tonkinson was a keen fossil hunter and amateur photographer.

A. Tonkinson and a relative pose with their motorcycles in the street. Sales of motor cycles boomed in the years following the 1914–1918 war.

The Heath family's car standing outside their house in Kingsfield Oval, Hartshill, c.1919. Very few families owned cars at this time.

A husband and wife pose in their car. Sales of cars quadrupled in Britain during the 1920s. At this time it was illegal to drive at more than 20 miles an hour. There was no driving test. This photograph is taken from a collection of glass negatives that were found in Todd's Chemist Shop, Burslem.

North Staffordshire Railway Company engine, 1858. The N.S.R. was formed in 1847 and by 1850 was operating 111 miles of track.

Steam engine at Stoke Station, c.1950. This informal scene was recorded by Charles Trelfa, an enthusiastic local photographer.

The Dolly Varden on the Trent and Mersey Canal, Stoke. This canal boat belonged to one of the directors of the North Staffordshire Railway Company.

Stoke-on-Trent Corporation steam traction roller, c.1900. This photograph was taken outside St. Peter's Chambers, Stoke.

Electric tram, with its driver and conductor. A poster advertises a production of the Scarlet Pimpernel at the Theatre Royal. The tram operatives are wearing thick overcoats to protect themselves from the weather.

Electric tram on Hartshill Bank, c.1905. The tramline from Stoke to Newcastle was not opened until 1904 because of a dispute about road widening.

Tram at the Meir terminus. This photograph is taken from a stereoscopic slide.

Single-deck bus at Woodhouse Street, Stoke, 1928. In order to meet the competition offered by the small bus companies operating in the area, the Tram Company introduced its own buses in 1928. This is a 37 seater bus made by Midland Red, which operated on the Stoke to Newcastle route.

Five

"Active Lads and Healthy Young Ladies"

Deaf girls' drill during sports day at the Mount School for the Blind and Deaf, October 1902. Great emphasis was placed on out-door activities at the school. The annual sports day was held in the school grounds until 1902 when the event, which had grown in scope and size, was moved to the football ground in Stoke.

Young athletes pose for a group portrait at the Hanley Flower Show, 1920s. Athletic displays were a regular feature at the flower show. William Poulson, one of the show's organisers, stands at the far right.

An unidentified cricket team flanked by a group of policemen, c.1900. This photograph was probably taken at the Stoke Cricket Club grounds, Station Road, Stoke. They had obviously ignored the advice of the *Photographic News* which urged cricket clubs to pose for action shots, as "no photographs are so uninteresting as those of cricket teams".

Members of the Christ Church Guild, Tunstall, c.1885. Sports played a central part in the guild's activities. This photograph was taken at around the time that extensions were being made to the church.

"Greetings from Burslem Cricket Club". This processional arch was erected by the cricket club as their contribution to the celebrations marking the official opening of Burslem Park on 1st September 1894. A huge procession of people, including the Police, Yeomanry, Fire Brigade, Post Office Workers and 7,000 School children, passed through the streets to the park.

Members of the Potteries Clarion Cycling Club and their bicycles, c.1904. The aim of the Clarion Club was to combine socialism with pleasure and healthy activity. It attracted a strong local following, and was based at the Glass Street Workingmen's Club, Hanley.

Group photograph of the Potteries Cycling Club, c.1900. Penny Farthing bicycles are just visible in the background in this badly faded photograph. The group's membership is exclusively male. By this time almost every town and village in the country had its own cycling club.

Members of the Potteries Clarion Cycling Club, 1925. This photograph was taken at the White Hart Inn, Eccleshall, during a weekend outing. The group includes E.R. Fuller, then manager of the local branch of Halford's Cycle Shop.

Swimming lesson, c.1924. The County Borough of Stoke-on-Trent offered swimming instruction for all school children aged twelve and upwards at five at five swimming centres. In 1923, 3,415 boys and girls were learning to swim. The borough employed twelve qualified swimming instructors.

Summerbank School Squadron Team, Tunstall, 1929. The four swimmers (A. Faraday, J. Copes, A. Heath and A. Breeze) pose with the Nash Peake Shield, which they had won in competition with other local School teams. Mr. W.H. Calkin (left) and Mr. F.W. Bridgwood look on.

Opposite: Boys swimming team, High Street School, Tunstall, 1931. The boys pose at the pool edge with the Nash Peake Shield and other trophies.

Stoke-on-Trent football club, wearing their "away strip", 1895. Tommy Clare, George Clawley and Jack Eccles stand at the back. Will Dickson is seated in the centre of the front row, with Joe Schofield on the far right. Joe Schofield, who had previously played for Hanley Hope Sunday School, left the team to become a school teacher in 1899. Tommy Clare later played for Port Vale.

The North Staffordshire Railway orphanage football team, 1910. There was a strong association between football and the railways. A number of early professional football players had a background as railway workers.

Longbridge Hayes football club, 1913/14 season. This was one of many teams representing the various small communities of the industrial villages within the Potteries.

Potteries Electric Traction Company teams, 1923. This photograph was taken at the team grounds on the corner of Shelton New Road and Victoria Road, Hartshill.

"Len Bridgett's Eleven", 1923. Stoke Ladies football team, pose with Ladies Cup. Alice Bridgett stands on the left, Len Bridgett to the right. Their grandaughter remembers that the team's activities were looked on with disapproval in some quarters. "Football was regarded by many people as unlady like".

Stoke Ladies football team, 1922. Len Bridgett who organised and managed the team stands on the right. The team, winners of the English Ladies Cup, included four of his daughters, Gladys (standing, far left), Lilian (seated, left), Ida (standing, far right) and Eva (seated right, on the ground). A crowd of 2,000 people watched the team beat Doncaster 3-1 in the final which was held at Cobridge Stadium.

Burslem Co-op Football Club, 1936. The coach, D. Smith, stands on the left, and W. Emmett, the Managing Director of the Burslem Co-operative Society is seated on the left. Seated on the right is A. Howard, Shops Inspector. The team were winners of the Haig and Haig Cup in 1936.

Stoke City "B" Team, 1944/45 season. Bob McGrory, the team Manager, stands on the right. Ted Wordley, coach, and Jack Phillips, Scout, crouch on the left and right of the players. The photograph was taken to celebrate the team's success in winning the Sentinel Cup.

Stoke City in action against Newcastle United, March 1949. This is one of a sequence of photographs taken from behind the goal posts at the Victoria Ground by Charles Trelfa, a keen chronicler of local life. It is shot from the Boothen end, and shows the Butler Street Stand.

The "Valiants" versus Walsall. This photograph was taken at the Old Recreation Ground off Bryan Street, Hanley, shortly before the club moved to the present Vale Park in 1950.

Billiards Room at the Hill Top Memorial Institute, Burslem, c.1935. William Cook takes aim, while Harry Moore and Cecil Hurd wait with their cues. John Alcock, a Wolstanton cycle dealer, is taking a shot on another table (far left). Sporting activities were often based in public houses and hotels. Churches and chapels provided alternative accommodation for leisure pursuits.

Junior cricketers, c.1950. Young cricketers at Broom Street School, Hanley, pose with their bats and trophies. The school kept a detailed photographic record of its pupils' activities.

The Doulton Fire Fighting Team spring into action, 1961. They were competing in the Stoke-on-Trent City Fire Brigade Fire Fighting Competition.

Six

Church and Chapel

Holy Trinity Church, Hartshill, c.1910. The church was built in 1842 and designed by George Gilbert Scott in the Early English style. Its construction was financed by the china manufacturer Herbert Minton, who lived nearby in Longfield cottage (which later became the Orthopaedic Hospital). A parsonage, school and school master's house, all designed by Scott, were also built at Minton's expense. The tram shelter in the foreground was erected c.1904.

St. Barnabas Ramblers Club, possibly in Newcastle Lane, Penkull, c.1900. These walkers were members of the congregation at St. Barnabas Church, which had been built on the corner of Fredrick Avenue and Oxford Street in 1899. They lived on the Allotments estate, an area which had itself recently been open fields crossed by footpaths.

Members of the Girls' Friendly Society, Hartshill, c.1910. The rector sits in the centre of this group photograph, which was taken in the grounds of the parsonage. The earliest formal organisations for young women, Girls' Friendly Societies often involved the female members of the vicar's family.

St. James' Church, Longton, c.1960. Built in 1833 and consecrated the following year, this is one of five large Anglican Churches that were built locally to provide places of worship for the rapidly growing urban population. These "Commissioners' Churches", as they were known, were largely financed from a national fund which had been set up by parliament in 1818.

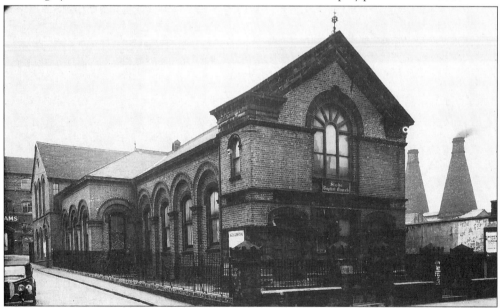

The Baptist Church, London Road, Stoke, c.1920. A poster advertises a special service for "Women's Sunday". The Church was built in 1853 and enlarged in 1879. It was financed from voluntary contributions and seated 500 people. The Baptists had a strong following among working people.

Swan Bank Chapel, Burslem, c.1890. When John Wesley first visited Burslem in 1760 he was struck in the head by a clod of earth. However, Methodism swiftly gained a strong following in the Potteries and a chapel was built in 1766. This was replaced in 1801 by Swan Bank Chapel, which was enlarged in 1816 to seat 1,290 people. The chapel was eventually replaced in 1971.

Providence Chapel, Town Road, Hanley, c.1910. Non-Conformity flourished in the Potteries. Providence Chapel was built in 1839 and replaced in 1924. A large Sunday School was built to the rear of the chapel.

Joseph Pointon's house, near Mow Cop, c.1890. In July 1801, Hugh Bourne, a carpenter, preached a sermon to a group of local Methodists in a field alongside Joseph Pointon's house. This was the beginning of the revivalist movement known as Primitive Methodism. "Our chapels", wrote Bourne, "were the coal-pit banks, or any other place; and in our conversation way, we preached the gospel to all, good or bad, rough or smooth".

An impromptu Primitive Methodist meeting at Mow Cop, 1907. In May 1807 an open air prayer meeting, attended by several thousand people, was held at Mow Cop. Two months later, the Methodist Conference ruled that camp meetings were "highly improper". Hugh Bourne refused to accept this ruling and was expelled from the Methodist Society. His followers went with him and Primitive Methodism was born. An anniversary meeting was held at Mow Cop one hundred years later.

The congregation at the Centenary Memorial Camp Meeting, Mow Cop, May 1907. Held on the same spot as the first camp meeting, this gathering attracted almost 100,000 participants.

"Number Three Preaching Stand", Mow Cop, May 1907. According to one eye witness, "The order, reverence, fervour, the praying, preaching, singing and testimonies can only be compared with those of Pentecost. It was a reconsecration of an already consecrated height".

The Jubilee Chapel, Tunstall, c.1906. The chapel, an important centre for Primitive Methodism, was refurbished in 1904 and was host for the Centenary conference in 1910.

The Trustees of Mow Cop Chapel, c.1910. This photograph was taken for the Souvenir booklet published to commemorate the centenary conference at Tunstall.

Hill Top Methodist Church, Burslem, 1937. A non-denominational Sunday School was established at the Wesleyan Chapel in 1787. The School's aim was "to instruct youth in useful learning". A bitter dispute arose when the chapel's trustees decided that the school should no longer teach reading and writing and in May 1836 the teachers were locked out of the premises. It was decided at a public meeting to build a new school and chapel and Hill Top opened the following year.

Hill Top Centenary Tea Meeting, April 1937. Around 400 local Methodists took part in this gathering, which was one of a number of events organised to celebrate the 100th anniversary of Hill Top Church.

A Ladies Sewing Meeting, Hill Top Methodist Church, 1937. This was one of many community activities organised by the church. Surprisingly, in 1896, the chapel trustees received a complaint from the Boys Brigade that their meetings were frequently interrupted by the sewing circle.

The choir at Hill Top Methodist Church, 1937. The organist, Mr.T.B. Lewis, is sitting in the middle of the second row.

A line of children wait with empty mugs, outside the congregational chapel in Caroline Street, Longton, April 1912. This photograph was taken during the coal strike, when the chapel was providing tea for families suffering hardship. The Chapel was described as being "more in the nature of a congregation hall than a church, being adapted to the character of work needed to be done in the district".

Trent Vale Church football club, 1920. Many local churches organised their own football teams. As many as a quarter of all the football clubs playing during the 1880s originated in religious organisations.

St. John the Baptist Church, Longton, c.1950s. This church had its origins in a small chapel which was built at Lane End in 1762, rebuilt in 1795 and substantially enlarged in 1828. Originally part of Stoke Parish, St. John's was given its own parish in 1868. Badly affected by mining subsidence, the church was demolished in 1979.

St. John the Baptist Church Choir, 1964. At this time the choir boasted 32 members (men and boys). The rector, Kenneth Cresswell, acted as choirmaster. Each year, the choirboys were treated to an outing to Llangollen, where they stayed for one night in the Youth Hostel.

Boundary Street Methodist Sunday School float, Hartshill, 1935. To celebrate the Silver Jubilee in June 1935, a procession of waggons, floats, bands and dancing troupes was organised. These Sunday School children are using a waggon which probably came from the coal yard at the end of Boundary Street.

A Roman Catholic Sunday School procession, Longton, c.1920s. These children probably belonged to the congregation of St. Gregory's Church, Heathcote Road.

Members of the choir, St. Andrew's Church, Sneyd Green, late 1960s. This informal shot was taken by Helen Trelfa.

Holy Trinity Church, Sneyd Parish, 1950s. Built in 1852 and used until the early 1950s, Holy Trinity was eventually closed as a result of mining subsidence and a dwindling congregation. A new church was opened in Hamil Road and the site acquired by Royal Doulton. It was demolished in 1959.

Seven

That's Entertainment

Pupils of the Mount School for the Blind and Deaf perform in their Christmas Show, 1900. The proceeds from the sale of tickets for the show were used to finance an annual trip to the seaside.

"A Wonderful Show". The *Sentinel* was highly impressed by the pupils' performance of *Red Riding Hood*, a short play written by the headmaster, Mr. A.J. Storey. The *Sentinel* reported that "the words of the dramatic sketches were spoken by deaf children who before coming to the school three years ago were dumb".

Concert Party, 1914–1918 war. This photograph showing a group of servicemen with an array of dummy instruments was found in the effects of a former soldier from Longton.

The Minstrel Mites performing *Robert Make-Airs*. This intriguing photograph was taken by S. Ellis of Lichfield Street, Hanley.

Aladdin and Out, Burslem, January 1932. This pantomime, produced by Mrs Bertie Wood, was put on by members of the Hill Top Methodist Church.

Harvey Haynes, aged seventeen. A young musician poses for the camera with his violin. There were many outlets for music-making in the Potteries. The home, the church, the park, the music hall, the concert hall and the public house all provided opportunities for musical activity.

Amateur actors George Leese and George Hammersley, January 1930. They are in costume as Norman and Prosper, two characters from the operetta *The Lilac Domino*, which was performed at the Grand Theatre, Hanley.

A scene from the final act of *The Lilac Domino*, performed by the Stoke-on-Trent Amateur Operatic and Dramatic Society. This was the Society's second production of the show, which in 1929 had won the National Operatic and Dramatic Association's Challenge Cup. The Society's musical director was John Cope, a well known figure in the Potteries musical scene.

The French Foreign Legion invade the stage of the Theatre Royal, Hanley, January 1933. The *Desert Song* was one of a number of ambitious productions staged by the Stoke-on-Trent Amateur Operatic and Dramatic Society. Founded in 1896, the society's earlier shows had included the first ever amateur production of *Castles in the Air*.

Members of the North Staffordshire Amateur Operatic Society, 1933. Founded in 1892, the Society specialised for many years in presenting Gilbert and Sullivan operas. During the 1930s the society brought a number of prestigious Drury Lane productions to the Potteries. The annual subscription to the society was ten shillings.

The Stoke-on-Trent Historical Pageant Choir in rehearsal, 1930. A spectacular pageant was held in Hanley Park in May 1930 to celebrate the bicentenary of Josiah Wedgwood's birth. A musical accompaniment was provided by a large choir, directed by John Cope.

Four Women from Hartshill relax backstage in their pageant costumes. Hundreds of people from around the Potteries took part in the production as actors, musicians and backstage workers.

Portland Vases on parade in Hanley Park. The pageant consisted of historical re-enactments. This is a scene from Episode Six which illustrated incidents in the life of Josiah Wedgwood. The Portland Vases appeared to Wedgwood in a dream!

The Queen of Ceramic Art. Lady Francis Joseph took on this role, with her two daughters as train bearers. She appeared in the final episode of the Pageant, alongside Old King Coal, Prince Gas and Princess Petroleum.

"Thomas Cooper addresses a crowd of Chartists". Cooper was one of the Chartist movement's most effective orators. For the Pageant, his role was taken by the local Labour M.P., Andrew Maclaren.

"Down with class rule and privilege". A film was made of the Pageant. This lively crowd scene shows the re-enactment of the 1842 Chartist disturbances in Hanley.

Waiting for the next dance. This photograph which shows an unidentified band on the stage at Tunstall Town Hall, was taken in 1938.

Workers' Playtime, 1948. This promotional photograph, showing a lunchtime dance at J. and G. Meakin's factory, was used as part of a recruitment campaign aimed at school leavers. The firm offered employees the use of a sports field " for cricket, bowls, and basket ball", as well as a subsidised staff canteen.

V.J. Celebration Dance, 1945. This strangely still photograph was taken at a dance organised for munitions factory workers at Biddulph.

Members of the Queensberry Road Music Club, Longton, 1950. A wide range of leisure activities, including music, drama, dance and sports, were organised at youth centres throughout the City in the post-war years. Young people paid ten shillings a year to belong to the Queensberry Centre. According to the Chairman of the Education Committee, Councillor Pemberton, the proliferation of youth clubs was largely responsible for "the diminishing number of juvenile delinquents in the City".

Skating rink carnival, Hanley, c.1910. Mr Tom Bew, the rink manager, stands on the right in a waiter's uniform. Bert Scott stands to his left. Frances Lovell stands behind a large bottle of Bass ale.

Harpfield Youth Club drama group, Hartshill, c.1950. The club met on Monday and Wednesday evenings at Harpfields County Modern School.

The Doulton Choir performs *Faust*, November 1966. Philip Ravenscroft (Mephistopheles) sings "The Song of the Golden Calf".

Making a noise. Children at Broom Street Nursery, Hanley, play with percussion instruments, c.1950.

Combined School choirs perform at the Victoria Hall, Hanley, 1952. On this occasion, Percy Rogers, Musical Director, and Dorothy Rowley, pianist, were joined by the conductor, John Barberolli. The choral tradition is still maintained in the City's music centres with regular performances at the Victoria Hall and other venues. The Victoria Hall was built as an extension to Hanley Town Hall in 1888. Its fine acoustics made the hall a popular venue with musicians, including the composer Elgar, who conducted a number of performances here.

Eight

The People's Parks

Mrs Emma Shelley on horseback in Queen's Park, Longton, c.1890. A wide carriage drive and three miles of walks were laid out in Queen's Park, which opened in July 1888. Although horses were welcome, bicycles, tricycles and dogs were banned from the park.

The Bandstand, Queen's Park, c.1890s. Bandstand concerts were expected to become "one of the greatest attractions of the park, and prove an irresistible inducement to the thousands of our weary toilers to shake off the atmosphere of the workshop and breathe the pure air of the people's park". However, in 1892, Longton Borough Council issued a notice "warning persons against dancing on the grass or otherwise causing damage during band concerts".

The Landing Stage, Queen's Park. The hire of a boat in 1899 was one shilling an hour for one or two people, with an extra charge of six pence for each additional person. For many local people, this was the equivalent of half a day's wages.

A fete in Queen's Park, 1890s. Longton Borough Council organised Whitsun fetes to raise income. Charges were generally waived for charitable events staged in the park. When the North Staffordshire Miner's Federation requested the use of the park in 1907 for their annual rally, however, they were asked to pay £100 and to agree to make good any damage.

The bridge and bowling pavilion, Queen's Park, c.1910. The sign in the foreground warns visitors to "Keep off the Grass". This is probably one of five dozen cast-iron notice plates which were brought for the park in 1889. The bowling green was laid out in 1906, but football and cricket were not allowed.

A commemorative display in Queen's Park, 1951. The parks department celebrated the Festival of Britain with this floral arrangement at Longton.

A Summer afternoon in Longton Park, c.1950. A small child sits on the steps in front of a miniature floral house.

The Aviary, Longton Park. A number of peacocks were kept here. "They were absolutely fantastic, walking about the park, opening up their feathers", recalled one former park worker.

"Success to Our Park", 1st September 1894. This ceremonial arch was erected at the entrance to Burslem Park for the opening celebrations. The park was laid out on "one of the most barren sites in the town, its surface composed principally of pit refuse". It took 70,000 loads of topsoil to cover the 22 acre site, which opened at a cost of £15,000. At the opening ceremony, the Mayor stated that it was "a red letter day in the history of the town. Burslem was setting the pace for the other pottery towns".

Park Keepers at Hanley Park. The Parks and Cemeteries Committee attempted to exercise strict control over the activities which took place in the City's parks. The park keepers were a symbol of authority, respected but often resented by local children. "You took notice of the Keep Off the grass Signs," remembers one resident. "You wouldn't dare stand on the grass in those days". Another recalls that, during the Hanley Flower Show, "lads would slip in between the railings to see the fireworks for free, but we'd run a mile if we saw a park keeper".

Hanley Town Prize Band on the balustrade at Burslem Park. Samuel Kirkham (far right) stands with his four sons, Tom, Enoch, George and Sam. Samuel died in 1916, but his sons survived the 1914–1918 War. George later became conductor of the Stoke-on-Trent Military Band, while Enoch played in the Collosseum Orchestra, Burslem.

Children in Cauldon Gardens, c.1905. The first section of Hanley Park to be completed, the Cauldon Grounds, were opened in July 1894. The design, by the young landscape architect Thomas Mawson, incorporated a lodge, conservatory, gates and ornamental fountains. Councillor Wood complained that too much money was being spent on the project.

The bowling green, Hanley Park. A large bowling green and a tennis lawn were included in Thomas Mawson's designs for Hanley Park. However, schools were not allowed to play football or cricket in the park until 1908. The pavilion and bandstand can be seen behind the Cauldon Canal, which bisects the park.

The organising committee, Hanley Horticultural Fete, September 1919, photographed at the Victories Hotel, Stoke. The fete was launched in 1897 in the belief that horticulture would prove an "improving" influence on local working people. The organisers believed that an appreciation of natural beauty would benefit both pottery workers and their employers.

Horse drawn carriages arrive for the Hanley Park fete, c.1900. A grand affair, the fete was held every July from 1897 until 1939.

Prize winners in the children's section, Hanley Park Horticultural Fete. Children at all the local Schools were encouraged to enter their home-grown plants. School parties were brought to the show to see the floral displays. A former pupil of Cauldon School recalls that he was more interested in Pat Collins' fair, which was on at the same time.

Pit ponies on display in Hanley Park. The annual horse parade, held until 1939, was a popular event. Shire horses, pit ponies, and decorated coal wagons paraded through the streets to the park for the judging.

The mayoral party relaxes at Hanley Flower Show, 1919. The Mayor, William Robinson stands on the left, holding a bouquet of flowers. Also pictured are William Poulson, Mr Farr (seated) and the Lady Mayoress.

A member of the Women's Land Army undergoes training in the greenhouse at Hanley Park. During the Second World War, women volunteers worked in the City's parks to maximise the use of available land for the war effort. Vegetables were planted in place of the usual floral displays.

A parks gardener inspects potted plants in the greenhouse.

The Conservatory at Hanley Park, c.1950. Built in 1893 at a cost of £879, the conservatory has now been demolished.

Norman Dracott (left) and Albert Carrall stand alongside their apprentice, Doug Bradbury, Queen's Park, Longton, c.1938. Norman Dracott worked in the park for 46 Years.

Electrical Exhibition stand at Hanley Park, late 1920s.

Left: Jack Beeston and Graham Garret in Etruria Park, 1937. Etruria Park had opened in 1904. Right: Jack Beeston and his Junior Cycle, bought when his father won the pools. The family were also treated to a holiday in Scarborough on the winnings!

142

Nine

Holidays and
Celebrations

The Market Place and Town Hall, Burslem, 1887. A huge crowd, including members of the yeomanry, the rifle volunteers and local friendly societies, gathered to celebrate Queen Victoria's Jubilee. A group of civic dignitaries watched the proceedings from the platform above the entrance arch.

Opposite: "God Save The King", 9th August 1902. The residents of Steel Street in Hartshill celebrated the coronation of Edward VII with a street party. The photograph was taken from Hartshill Road.

Bratt and Dyke's store, Trinity Street, Hanley, 1897. Oliver Bratt and Henry Dyke had built their store on the site of the former Roebuck Inn during the previous year. Here it is decorated to celebrate Queen Victoria's Diamond Jubilee.

May Day celebrations, Wolstanton Marsh, 1905. A group of girls, wearing their best pinafore dresses, dance around the maypole.

Dresden Church of England Infant School, May Festival, c.1920. The photograph was taken in the School yard.

Bonfire at Fenton Manor, 1911. This was one of two bonfires built at Fenton to mark the coronation of King George V in June 1911. According to the *Sentinel*, "the flames could be seen for a distance of several miles". The celebrations also included a 21-gun salute, a procession of 5,000 schoolchildren, and sporting events in the Manor field.

Hartshill Pageant, c.1913. This annual event took the from of a parade through the streets of Hartshill, followed by a carnival in Gorton's Farm fields. The pageant was held from 1909 until the mid-1920s.

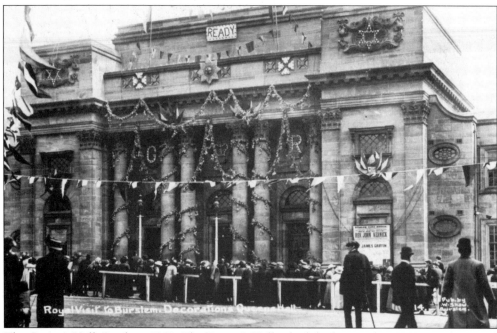

The Queen's Hall, Burslem, 1913. The Queen's Hall, which had opened in 1911, was decorated in honour of King George V and Queen Mary, who visited the town on 22nd April 1913.

"Meet the Quins", Silver Jubilee celebrations, Hartshill, June 1935. A procession of decorated carts, dancing troupes, bands and people wearing fancy dress paraded through the streets. This photograph was taken at the Drill Hall parade ground, off Wilfred Place.

Coronation street party, 1953. Young and old residents of Mollart Street, Hanley, celebrate the accession of Elizabeth II. The photograph shows members of the Beech, Brookes, Clarke and Massey families.

Albert Tonkinson (second from right) and friends pose with their bicycles. The handlebars are decorated with garlands of spring flowers.

A family outing with bicycles, c.1910. A kettle is being boiled on a primus stove. Bicycling provided greater freedom for those families able to afford it.

Potteries Clarion Club gathering, May 1910. The first Clarion Cycling Club had been formed in 1894. By 1896 there were 120 clubs, with a membership of 7,000 people.

Members of the Clarion Club relax at their Club House. Sponsored by the socialist Clarion Fellowship, the club houses were fore-runners of youth hostels.

Easter outing for children, Bloor's Garage, Hartshill Road, 1926. During a period of high unemployment, many local families subsisted in poverty. Various free events were organised for the children of the area, including this trip to the seaside.

The Hartshill Queen and her attendants, c.1937. An annual garden party was held on the green at the corner of Albany Road and the Avenue. A "Queen" was chosen for this event and also entered in the Queen of Queens Competition, organised on behalf of the North Staffordshire Infirmary. This photograph shows Gladys Jackson as the Hartshill Queen.

The School Rose Queen and her attendants, Spring 1957. This photograph was probably taken in the yard of Cannon Street Infants School, Hanley.

Milton Church Queen, 1964. This photograph was taken in the grounds of St. Philip and St. James Church, Milton, by Helen Trelfa.

Works outing, 1902. This photograph shows a group of workers from Pointon's China Factory, Norfolk Street, Hanley, enjoying an excursion.

Employees of the Co-operative Wholesale Pottery Works, Longton, pose in their "Sunday best" outfits during their annual gathering.

Chapmans Works outing, c.1950. A group of pottery workers wait for the coaches to a arrive. Mr G.D. Wild is standing in the centre of the second row. The photograph was taken at the corner of Sutherland Road and London Street, looking up towards the Park Place Works.

Christmas Decorations, Barratt's Ltd, Burslem, December 1947. This promotional photograph, taken in the firm's new decorating workshop, was designed to attract young recruits to the workforce.

RUDYARD LAKE, NR. LEEK.

R-20

Boating at Rudyard Lake, c.1905. This was a popular destination for many local families, who could not afford to travel very far.

ENTRANCE TO TRENTHAM PLEASURE GARDENS

The entrance to Trentham Pleasure Gardens, c.1920s. Trentham Gardens, with its large open-air swimming pool, ballroom and boating lake, attracted large crowds of Potteries people.

Hanley Wakes, Parliament Row, 1898. For a week each year the centre of Hanley was taken up with "a fearful and wonderful collection of itinerant and other displays". These included swings and roundabouts, steam organs, shooting galleries, boxing booths and coconut shies.

Swingboats, trapeze frame and marquees, Longton Park, c.1900. Fairs and fetes were organised in Longton Park in order to raise money to pay off its debts.

Hanley Wakes, Regent Road, 1st August 1927. These four photographs are taken from a film which was made to record this popular annual event. The shows were organised by Pat Collins, the Walsall-based fairground entrepreneur.

A showman and monkey entertain the crowds at the Regent Road Fairground. The wakes were relocated here in 1923 following a lengthy campaign to have them removed from the town centre. The Shows were "a Pandemonium and there was nothing particularly edifying for the people", complained Alderman Elliot. "If the people wanted the fairs, let them find a more convenient place for it".

A crowded scene at the fairground. A placard advertising Nocetti's Original Ices is visible below the swingboats.

Children enjoy the fairground rides at Regent Road. Although some "respectable" people regarded the wakes as a noisy nuisance, the fair brought welcome colour and excitement to the town. Regent Road remained the focus for annual festivities until the 1960s.

The boys and girls of Burnwood County Secondary School Choir sing at the School's opening ceremony in 1960. The school was officially opened by the Labour leader Hugh Gaitstell.